NORTH AMERICAN TRACTION

The Impressions of an English Railfan

DAVE HEWITT

AMBERLEY

First published 2025

Amberley Publishing
The Hill, Stroud
Gloucestershire, GL5 4EP

www.amberley-books.com

ISBN 978 1 3981 2859 0 (print)
ISBN 978 1 3981 2860 6 (ebook)

British Library Cataloguing in Publication Data.
A catalogue record for this book is available from the British Library.

Typesetting by SJmagic DESIGN SERVICES, India.
Printed in the UK.

Appointed GPSR EU Representative:
Easy Access System Europe Oü, 16879218
Address: Mustamäe tee 50, 10621, Tallinn, Estonia
Contact Details: gpsr.requests@easproject.com, +358 40 500 3575

CONTENTS

CANADA

My most abiding memory of July 1966 is not that England won the World Cup, but that I flew for the first time. I went to visit my sister who after she got married in 1964 immediately emigrated to Canada and settled in Timmins, Ontario. My father bought a flight from Manchester to Montreal whilst I purchased a train ticket to Timmins – well, I was only a student at that time. The feeling of crossing the tarmac and climbing the steps into the front of a Boeing 707 was amazing. Only the Beatles did this, right? Nobody I knew had ever flown, yet here I was, sitting in a window seat looking at clouds. Very soon we landed at Prestwick in Scotland, to pick up more passengers! I looked out as steps were rolled out to the front door of the plane enabling a small group of passengers to board and take their seats. I also watched horrified as a man strolled out with a long ladder, leant it against the aircraft's wing and climbed up to one of the engines with something akin to an oversized screwdriver. I sat transfixed, eyes on the engine, as he worked. I couldn't take my eyes off that wing, even after he left and the plane was airborne – when was the engine going to fall off? My reverie was broken by the captain announcing that we would be late arriving in Montreal, so late that I would not have enough time to get into the city to catch my train. I got the attention of one of the air hostesses and explained my situation, adding that should I miss the train, I would have to charge the cost of a hotel room and a fresh ticket to BOAC. (How I found the nerve to say that at the age of nineteen I will never know!) She went away. On her return she invited me into the cockpit to speak with the captain, who asked if I was catching the Super Continental which left Montreal at 5 p.m. When I confirmed that this was my train, he smiled and said that things would be fine, as it stopped at Montreal airport at 5.20 p.m. He would instruct the authorities to ease my passage through arrival formalities to ensure I caught my train. He was true to his word. I was first off the plane and was stood on the station platform by 5 p.m. The train took me to North Bay, Ontario, where I had to change trains and take a sleeper to Timmins. It was just like the movies. An attendant showed me my compartment and promised to wake me half an hour before reaching Timmins. He did, bringing along a welcome cup of hot coffee to start the day. Fifty years later and North Bay is my annual destination as family have settled there, with grandsons to indoctrinate into a love of railways.

My sister moved around Canada, ending up in Vancouver. Because of her ill health I used to visit her, taking a flight to Seattle, driving through Washington, Idaho, Montana and British Columbia on the way to her home. I discovered the famous Morant's Curve, named after Canadian Pacific photographer Nicholas Morant, who photographed it in the 1940s. On my first visit to that iconic spot I remained for three hours with only a photograph of a bear on the tracks for my troubles. The second time I stayed for eight hours before I got a picture. I stood by the track, camera poised, eager for that famous image. After a few minutes a couple joined me track side, others followed until after half an hour there was quite a crowd. Someone asked me, 'Hey, bud, what have you seen, a bear maybe?' 'Nope,' I replied, 'I'm waiting for a train.' The crowd dispersed grumbling but within an hour the same thing would happen again. Seven crowds later, I got my picture. Railway photography in America has always seemed to me to be just like fishing.

Ontario

Above: Train 451 is a daily turn from Toronto to North Bay with freight traffic for the ONR and the OVR, the two railway companies based in the town, who use the much-reduced Canadian Pacific freight yard as a centre for their operations. CN 8832 (EMD SD70-M2) is on lead as it approaches the crossing of Lake Nosbonsing Road, south of North Bay.

Opposite: CN 2795 (GE ES44AC) leads a stack train over the trestle bridge at Parry Sound on the Canadian Pacific-built line from Toronto to Sudbury. CN and CPR both use this line to head West; the CN line, which is further inland, is used for east-bound trains.

Ontario Northland Railway 2121 (EMD SD70M) leads train 214 out of North Bay for Englehart on the same track on which I rode a sleeper back in 1966. The ONR used to run a daily passenger service to Toronto, called the Northlander, but it ceased in 2012. There are currently plans to restore the service in 2026.

ONR 2104 (EMD ED75I) approaches Widdicombe Station Road, north of North Bay, with train 213, the return working from Englehart.

ONR 2021 (EMD SD70M) passes through the town of Cobalt and the remains of the Right of Way Mine. This area was a major centre for the mining of silver in the early twentieth century and the town gets its name from the metal which is a by-product of silver production.

Ottawa Valley Railway 3407 (EMDSD40-2) heads the daily train from North Bay to Temiscaming. The other service operated by the railway runs to Sudbury on Mondays, Wednesdays and Fridays. On my first visit to North Bay, I called into the offices to enquire as to the timing of the trains and was amazed to find so few operated. However, regular visits to the railway led to my grandsons and I riding this train for 60 miles to Mattawa, an experience none of us will forget.

Photographed the day after our trip, the locomotive we rode, OVR 2112 (EMD SD-38), rolls past Camey on its way to Temiscaming.

The three times a week service to Sudbury terminates in the Canadian Pacific yard. OVR 2054 (EMD SD-38) is on point crossing over the Wanapitei River on the outskirts of Sudbury.

Huron Central Railway 3010 (EMD GP40-2) heads a pickup freight over the Spanish River Dam at Espanol, moving towards the exchange sidings. This was a daily service from Sudbury but no longer operates due to the closure of the mill it served.

Huron Central's exchange sidings at McKerrow, a few miles north of Espanola. The railway is based in Sudbury and runs a daily freight to Sault Ste. Marie where it connects with Canadian National before returning to Sudbury.

British Columbia

Above: Roosville is the port of entry from Idaho into British Columbia and from there Highway 93 heads north eastwards towards Banff in Alberta via Radium Hot Springs, where there is a junction with Highway 95. This meanders north alongside the Columbia River and the Canadian Pacific Railway to meet the Trans-Canada Highway at the railway town of Golden, providing many opportunities for the photographer. Canadian Pacific 9827 (GE AC4400CW) with an empty coal train heading south alongside the Columbia River illustrates what is possible.

Opposite: The Agawa Canyon Tour Train, based in Sault Ste. Marie, takes passengers to a canyon which is only accessible by train. F40 106 brings its train load of passengers back to the SOO in what is the most popular season for travel, the autumn.

Above: An unidentified Canadian Pacific locomotive with a long train of empty coal wagons taken at Canal Flats situated at the southern end of Lake Columbia which is the source of the Columbia River.

Opposite: Radium Hot Springs. A very long train of empty coal wagons rumbles south with unidentified Canadian Pacific locomotives at the head and centre of the train.

Above: The area around Spillimacheen is particularly good for photography as the track follows Highway 95 almost into Golden. It is here that I picked up CPR 9827 (GE AC4400CW) for the first time. Not having a scanner meant that once I came across a train, I would chase it as far as I could, clicking as I went.

Opposite: CPR 8520 (GE AC4400CW) in the spring, north of Spillimacheen, with the inevitable train of empty coal wagons.

8520
8520
8520

Above: The town of Golden is on the main Trans-Canada Highway, Highway 1. Heading east towards Vancouver, the first major rail centre encountered is at Revelstoke where a rail bridge crosses the Columbia River. CPR 9584 (GE AC4400CW) is the first of three locomotives with an eastbound empty grain train.

Opposite: Highway 1 westbound eventually reaches the Thomson River Valley with CPR and CN tracks on either side of the river. A CPR empty coal train heads east through the spectacular scenery.

Above: Canadian National 2511 (GE C44-9WL) has the lead with a full coal train in the Thomson River Valley. The two rail companies share the tracks so that everything heading east uses one line; the other line is reserved for trains heading west.

Opposite: Looking more like a model railway, a Canadian National stack train crosses the Fraser River on one of the two bridges at Cisco heading for Kamloops.

East of Golden, on Highway 1, is the town of Field where trains wait for their turn to go through the Spiral Tunnels which were built to lessen the grade through Kicking Horse Pass. Canadian Pacific 8636 (AC4400CW) leads its grain train into the yard after negotiating the tunnels.

Canadian Pacific 8739 (GE ES44AC) is westbound with a grain train as it approaches Morant's Curve, found on the Alberta, BC border.

Was it worth the wait? Canadian Pacific 8619 (AC4400CW) with a stack train at Morant's Curve with no bears or tourists in sight.

UNITED STATES

Chicago

In 2006 my friend Alan said he wanted to do a road trip in America. Unfortunately, he couldn't drive, so did I fancy going with him? His idea was to do as much of Route 66 as possible in two weeks and I readily agreed. The simple itinerary began to change as we made plans. A trip to Memphis to pay our respects to Elvis, a visit to the Grand Canyon, train rides on some of the heritage lines along the route and a flight home from Denver were added to flesh out the skeleton of driving the Mother Road. In the back of my mind, I thought that I might be able to write an article about our journey, so I emailed the various attractions we planned to visit. The internet twenty years ago was far more innocent than today, and my requests were treated with respect and a desire to help. My email to Graceland asked what restrictions there were regarding writing and photographing Elvis' home. After a lengthy conversation Alan and I were allowed to wander around the house by ourselves with no other tourists present! The response from the Grand Canyon Railway to my question of where I could photograph their train resulted in a three-day stay at their hotel, with meals and a train trip to the Grand Canyon, as guests of the railway. Other freebies, though not so magnanimous, were forthcoming and it was with great excitement that we drove to Manchester to fly to Chicago.

'And what is the purpose of your visit to the United States?' asked the agent from Homeland Security, after I had checked in with American Airways. 'Holiday,' I said, 'Route 66.' Pointing to a chart to his right he enquired, 'Do you have any of these in your luggage?' On the chart were depicted various weapons, ranging from sub machine guns to pistols, swords to machetes and a round black shape with a fuse adorned with the word BOMB. 'This is ludicrous,' I thought, but out loud I replied 'No, but can I ask you a question?' 'Sure, but don't expect an answer.' 'Well, I mean, has anyone admitted to having a bomb in their luggage?' He thought for a second and then said, 'I am more interested as to why you would ask that question?' 'Just my sense of humour,' I said, not digging the hole I was in any deeper. He let me go. On arrival in Chicago, my luggage had been searched. My friend Fred and I flew to Chicago a year later with American Airlines; my luggage was searched once more. After that I travelled with Delta!

Ten years later and I drove into Chicago to visit my former neighbour Darren, discovering as I did so the delights of being in lane 7 of an eight-lane toll road during the rush hour with the cash toll booth on lane 1. Darren took me on the El for a trip downtown, hence the next three pictures.

302
5005

Above: A northbound Brown line train for Kimball crosses the Chicago River in Downtown Chicago.

Opposite: A westbound train on the Pink line of Chicago's elevated subway, better known as the El, at Clinton station.

CNA
STOP

Washington

I have flown to Seattle five times and have yet to see the sun! No wonder Washington's unofficial nickname is the Evergreen State for there has been rain on every one of my visits. The primary reason for my first two trips was to call upon my sister in nearby British Columbia; for the remainder of my stays I was a tourist. I went to the Grand Coulee Dam in the rain, drove around the Olympic peninsula in fog, went up the Space Needle in Seattle to view the clouds, called next door to the Museum of Pop Culture to look at the Jimi Hendrix exhibit only to find it had been lent to a museum in another part of the country. A brochure informed me that Mount Rainier was wonderful with a mountain meadow that had inspired poets for generations, so I went, even though it was late October, and it was raining. As the road climbed up the mountain it seemed to get colder with every bend in the road and when I pulled into a layby to let a snowplough go past, I decided that I really should be chasing trains.

After my third visit to my sister, I headed south, towards Oregon, and discovered the Columbia River Gorge. What a fabulous area for the railfan: stupendous scenery, a wide river with BNSF trains on the Washington side and Union Pacific operating on the south side in Oregon. As well as the railway tracks following the riverbank there was also a road either side which gave access to the trains which seemed to come every ten minutes. This was an added bonus for me because I never knew when a train was coming. American railfans have scanners which allow the user to follow the path of any given train. I didn't have one and what's more to the point I don't think I would be able to use one, so I had to come up with a plan.

After checking into a motel and having something to eat I would spend the evening with Google Earth and a large-scale map of the state which showed the railways. Google Earth was used to find suitably scenic locations and the map to work out routes from one shot to another which would enable me to get ahead of the train no matter from which direction it appeared. It sounds good in theory but what was not known was the frequency of the traffic. If I was lucky, I would pick up a train within thirty minutes and have several different shots in the camera before I had to let it go. If fate was against me, I could stand there all day and get nothing. As I said earlier, just like fishing.

The Columbia River Gorge therefore was something special; I never had to stand for any length of time before a train came. The remaining pictures in this section which are not in the Gorge are all down to patience or pure luck.

Opposite: The Chicago skyline dwarfs the South Shore line train from South Bend, Indiana, as it approaches the Millennium station terminus.

Above: BNSF 5432 (GE C44-9W) leads a freight past the Avery Recreational Area Washington along the northern bank of the Columbia River with Mount Hood in the distance on the Oregon side.

Opposite: BNSF 4761 (GE C44-9W) leads at stack train west along the Columbia River east of Stevenson, Washington.

J.B. HUNT
4761
4761
BNSF

On the Washington side unknown BNSF locomotives lead an auto train towards the crock of gold at the John Day Dam which straddles the Columbia River.

BNSF 614 (GE C44-9W), in Sante Fe livery, crosses the girder bridge at Stevenson in charge of a mixed freight. The bridge was replaced several years ago with a more functional, less-pleasing structure.

I stumbled on this location by pure chance as I was driving towards Spokane and took a diversion into Sprague. There was a second field with a mixture of vintage cars and lorries but that wasn't close to the railway. CP 8653 (GE AC4400CW) is at the head of a southbound oil train.

Amtrak 467 (Cascades EMD F59PHI) departs Bellingham with an evening train for Vancouver.

Arizona

Alan and I left Chicago on Interstate 55 which had been built, for the most part, on the old Route 66. The weather was dismal, grey clouds blotting out the sun, and Illinois was flat and monotonous. Not a great start to our adventure. We were heading for Memphis and a date with Elvis. As we headed south the weather changed, the sun driving away the clouds. The journey became more interesting as we turned off the Interstate onto Highway 61, the road used by southern bluesmen travelling to Chicago hoping for a recording contract. It was on this road that bluesman Robert Johnson was supposed to have met the Devil at a crossroads and sold his soul for two years of wealth and fame. We never came across this infamous spot, but we did get to Graceland to photograph Elvis' home before making the long cross-country trip to Arizona and a ride on a steam train to the Grand Canyon.

Our first stop, after Memphis, was at Clinton, Oklahoma, after over 500 miles of non-stop driving. We checked into a motel and were asked if we wanted a meal because the restaurant was closing within the hour. We were tired so we gave it a try; Alan had catfish whilst I had a steak. We were served by two young women who, every five minutes or so, came and asked if everything was alright. After the sixth visit to our table I questioned them as to why they kept coming with the same enquiry. 'Well, sir,' one of them said, 'It's your accent. I reckon that if you spoke to any American women for thirty minutes you could have your way with her!' I was speechless. I am no Cary Grant; I'm from the West Midlands!

Arizona was everything I had hoped it would be and more. For someone brought up on imported black-and-white cowboy shows from America in the 1950s, it was a return to my childhood – but in colour. We travelled on Interstate 40, which had replaced Route 66, but there were plenty of stretches of the old road on which to drive and many interesting sights to visit. There were the Petrified Forest and the Painted Desert National Parks, in Holbrook there was a motel consisting of concrete wigwams and in Winslow there was a corner to stand on. The Interstate followed the railway for many miles across Arizona and it seemed as though we saw a mile-long freight train every fifteen minutes. I began to pay them some attention; I would have to return as a railfan, which I did, several times.

Opposite: It's May, a Sunday, and a BNSF locomotive at the rear of a coal train rounds Dogfish Point, south of Bellingham, at dusk heading for the terminal at Tsawwassen, BC.

FLAGSTAFF
6652

Above: BNSF 7875 (GE ES44DC) heads an eastbound stack train through Holbrook, raising dust on a hot afternoon. The Apache Railway tracks are on the left.

Opposite: BNSF 6652 (GE ES44C4) is at the front of a consist of eight locomotives as it passes westbound through Flagstaff station.

BNSF 7303 (GE ES44DC) at the head of five locomotives climbs out of Seligman with a stack train bound for California.

With a Sante Fe heritage unit behind, BNSF 5253 (GE C44-9W) runs an eastbound oil train out of Flagstaff.

81
81
Apache Railway
99
The Apache Railway

Above: BNSF 7043 (GE ES44C4) catches the evening light as it crosses a relic of the Santa Fe with a freight in Kingman Canyon.

Opposite: The Apache railway runs for 38 miles from Holbrook to Snowflake. One of its operations is car storage and here Apache railway 81 (ALCO Century 420) is hauling empty wagons away from Holbrook.

Early morning in Kingman Canyon and a southbound stack train has BNSF 6577 (GE ES44C4) at the head of three locomotives.

Michigan

If I wasn't chasing rustlers, train robbers and having a shoot-out at the OK Corral as a boy, I was rushing about shouting 'Book 'em, Dano' and 'message received, 10 4' in the style of the American police as depicted in 1950s cop shows such as *Highway Patrol*, *Hawaii Five-0* and *Dragnet*. I never thought at that time that I would ever encounter an American law-enforcement officer, but I did – three times that I can remember, twice in Michigan.

The state of Michigan is divided into the Upper and Lower Peninsular by the waterways that make up the Great Lakes. I always entered from Sault Ste. Marie, Canada, across a magnificent border bridge into Sault Ste. Marie, USA, which is in the Upper Peninsular and took the Interstate 75 towards the Lower Peninsular before taking a right, heading west for Green Bay in Wisconsin. The land is flat and the road is straight, cutting through endless swathes of trees, all seemingly of the same species and height. After ninety minutes of a boring drive I would make a stop at Engadine, twenty or so houses around a gas station and a railroad line. After making use of the restroom, I would take a walk to the track in the hope of a train. I only ever caught one, a coal train heading for the large yard in Sault Ste. Marie, Canada, which had left Gladstone, Michigan, three hours before and which would be my next stop.

The town is found on the shore of Lake Michigan and boasts a superior Subway overlooking the Canadian National yard. I find that a toasted 6-inch Italian beef sandwich tastes much better when there is train activity to go with it. Once, whilst having my lunch, I noticed that a train was ready to depart for Canada. I drove quickly to where the line crosses a residential road, parked and took my duffel bag with camera and lenses to the line to find a spot for a picture. I decided to use the 80-200 lens so put the 24-70 in the bag at my feet. The train approached, a car drew to a halt at the crossing; I took the picture and waited for the train to pass. It was a long one and the guy in the car began chatting, the conversation continuing after the last coal truck had vanished. Finally, he drove off, and I walked to my car and headed south. It took a full thirty minutes before I realised I hadn't picked up my bag. I returned to find that it was missing. I found the police station and explained what had happened. The officer didn't hold out much hope but promised to text me a week later with any news. I did receive a message to say that no one had handed in my bag but by this time I had been to a camera shop in Green Bay and purchased an expensive replacement lens. I didn't get a discount because of my accent but he did give me a hundred-dollar camera bag to carry the lens in.

A few miles further south is Escanaba, home to the Escanaba and Lake Superior Railroad, a short line running from the Upper Peninsular to Green Bay. On my last visit to Escanaba, I was driving in the inside lane of a congested dual carriageway when there was a loud bang and the offside wing mirror flew onto the top of the bonnet. The car that had overtaken me immediately pulled into my lane as the sound of a police siren rent the air. The police car escorted us both into a side road before the officer took statements. It transpired that he was an out-of-town policeman heading for a conference and had been driving behind me when the incident occurred. There were no '10 4s' or 'Book 'em'. A short interview and his card with a website address which, by the next day, would have dashcam footage of the accident. There was no film of the old and quite drunk lady driver.

The third meeting? Well, that was on my first trip with Fred. We were going to a baseball game in Denver. I had parked the car in a vacant lot close to Coors Field stadium and had no idea how to get onto Interstate 25, which was our destination after the game, so I asked a policeman. He was how we imagine American cops to be: overweight, almost bursting out of his uniform, a gun and truncheon strapped to his waist with a large cigar butt in his mouth. I asked how to access the Interstate, he gave me directions and, when he discovered I was English a lengthy conversation ensued about the merits, or otherwise, of Tony Blair and George Bush, which only ended because Fred needed the restroom.

Left: E & LSPR 1200 (EMD-SW8) with a train of grain wagons in Escanaba. The railroad has many stretches of line such as this which are used to store wagons belonging to other railroad companies.

Opposite: CN 8013 (EMD SD70M-2) leaves Gladstone with a coal train for Canada. It was here that I forgot to pick up my duffel bag after taking this picture.

E & LSPR 501 (EMD S40-2) at Bark River with a train from Green Bay for Escanaba on the main CN line from Canada to Green Bay.

A further 10 miles on from Bark River there is a junction at Powers with a branch line to Quinnesec along which Canadian National run a daily pickup freight which I have been fortunate to photograph several times. CN 5436 (EMD SD60) heads west past the small Vietnam War Museum at Hermansville with a westbound freight.

The Vietnam War Museum again as BCRAIL 4616 (GE C40-8M) returns from Quinnesec with a freight for Powers and Gladstone.

On the outskirts of Hermansville, CN 2655 (GE C44-9W) with the return working for Powers is ahead of the approaching storm.

Engadine and the only time I ever saw a train on the line. BNSF 6206 (GE ES44 AC) with a coal train for Sault Ste. Marie rides the roller-coaster. US railways never seem to do cuttings.

California and Oregon

When I visited these two states I was still in tourist mode, concentrating on heritage lines of which there are several. Fred came to California and although he liked riding trains, he wasn't that keen on hanging around for a train to turn up, so instead we went to Yosemite, Lake Tahoe, San Francisco, Monterey and an amazing little town called Lone Pine which was the back lot for Hollywood film companies. It was here that all the TV shows I had seen as a boy were filmed: the *Lone Ranger*, *Hopalong Cassidy* and the rest. Fascinating!

My week in Oregon was divided between two heritage lines and a tour of the state, taking in Crater Lake, the deepest lake in America, though I didn't see much of it due to the smoke from a forest fire which also interfered with my shots of the Mount Hood Railroad. Giant redwoods in Northern California were ticked off the bucket list, as was the beautiful Oregon Pacific coastline which took two days of driving to take it all in, but there was time for some train photography.

Oregon from the Washington side of the Columbia River Gorge with an unidentified pair of UP locomotives working a stack train eastwards.

Above: I am on the Riverside Trail east of the Dalles to photograph UP 8508 (EMD SD70Ace) at the front of a trio of locomotives hauling an eastbound stack train.

Opposite: UP 8296 (EMD SD9043MAC) with a westbound grain train passes through a glowing Columbia River Gorge close to the Dalles.

8296

The Moo, Port of Tillamook Bay 101 (EMD GP9), which was built in 1956 and is the only locomotive in the USA to be painted in the livery of a cow. I found it in a siding close to Garibaldi in Oregon along with 6139 (EMD SD9). Both are now at the Oregon Scenic Railway.

Overlooked by Mount Shastra, UP 4866 (EMD SD70M) crosses the California–Oregon border heading north in late evening sunshine.

A Californian sunset over BNSF's Barstow yard as a freight eases its way west.

In the early twentieth century, when long-distance rail travel was becoming popular, hotels and restaurants were built at strategic points along important routes to supply food and rest for the traveller. They were named Harvey Houses after their inventor Fred Harvey, and one still survives in Barstow. It has been converted into the Western America Railroad Museum but it had closed by the time Fred and I arrived. It did prove to be a decent vantage point to photograph the yard in the setting sun.

Tehachapi Loop, completed in 1876 to enable trains to climb up the Tehachapi Pass and still going strong. Approximately fifty trains a day negotiate the loop, but there were none on the day Fred and I called. We had to return the following day to catch sight of this BNSF stack train climb up the pass.

BNSF 7779 (GE ES44DC) on the approach to the loop from the eastern side.

BNSF

New Mexico and Arizona (Again)

Alan and I, still not believing what we had heard the hight before, left Clinton the next morning to drive into New Mexico, which we found to have some good stretches of Route 66 complete with relics from the time it was America's Main Highway. Route 66 changed its course many times over the years, and we chose the 1937 route which went via the state capital, Sante Fe. At breakfast I had been looking at some brochures I had found in the motel foyer and suggested that we take Highway 14 from Sante Fe to Albuquerque as it looked interesting, promising a ghost town. Los Cerillos was the ghost town; in fact, it was a cowboy ghost town and had been used for the filming of *Young Guns II* back in the 1980s. We wandered along dusty streets, walked on wooden boardwalks past empty hitching rails for horses and came upon a bar with a pickup parked outside. There was a guy inside who leant out of his window and said, 'Hey, that's a fancy camera, who ya working for?' 'The *London Times*,' I replied. 'Well,' he said, 'you had better come to my girl's place. It's called Tiny Town, just on the right when you head south on 14, we've had many reporters visit over the years. Tattooed Mary would make you very welcome. Why, here she is now.' A middle-aged lady appeared from the bar. Slight, wearing a shirt and shorts and with many tattoos, the most beguiling of which were the strands of barbed wire twisting up her legs, she said to the guy, 'They got no whisky, say who are these?' 'Couple of fellers from England. They're calling in when they leave here.' He turned to us with an open paper bag, 'Want some grits?' he asked and drove off when we declined.

Alan wondered 'Are we going?' 'No', I replied and got in the car and headed south past what must have been Tiny Town but resembled more of a junk yard. A few miles further on we came to Madrid which was full of hustle and bustle as a movie was being shot there. We stopped and talked to a security guard who was preventing people from entering the set. 'It's a film starring John Travolta,' he explained, 'called Wild Hogs. Say are you from England? I really want to go there.' I asked him why. 'I want to go to Wooostertershire,' he said tripping over the name of the English county. 'I want to stand outside Robert Plant's house; I am a big Led Zeppelin fan. I would love to meet him.' Just then there came the sound of a vehicle drawing up behind me and a male voice said, 'I see you didn't get to Tiny Town.' We left.

But I returned years later and managed to get pictures south of Albuquerque and along the Arizona section of Route 66.

Opposite: Route 66 country on the border of California with Arizona. BNSF 7043 (GE ES44C4) heads a stack train on the way to Kingman.

Storm clouds are gathering behind BNSF 8167 (GE ES44C4) as it heads south avoiding Albuquerque, with a stack train.

With the storm inching ever closer, BNSF 7363 GE ES44DC runs southbound parallel to Highway 6.

Above: Storm clouds are now gathering over this BNSF stack train travelling south from Albuquerque and I would meet up with them when I reached the Painted Desert.

Opposite: BNSF 4143 (GE C44-9W) at the head of four locomotives brings a stack train into West Winslow under the shadow of the San Francisco Peaks.

Above, opposite and overleaf: Two unidentified stack trains glide past Meteor City, an abandoned relic from the days when Route 66 was the road to travel. Many such buildings remain on the roadside mostly abandoned.

BNSF

HERE
IT IS

Opposite: But the Jack Rabbit Trading Store still operates. All along the 2,000-mile length of Route 66 the enterprising owner placed images of the rabbit together with details of how far it was to the store – a very early example of roadside advertising. Citirail 1205 (GE ES44AC) doesn't stop.

Right: Indulge me. Heat haze distorts an approaching BNSF stack train as it nears the Harvey House, La Posada, in Winslow.

Along Route 66 between Kingman and Seligman, a vantage point allows a view of an oil train with BNSF 4318 (GE C44-9W) at the head.

FAILURE (PART I): NEW ENGLAND

When railfanning there are good days and bad days. Take two or more excellent pictures and the day has been successful, below that benchmark it has been a failure. From my experience Mondays always have the potential to be bad because I believe that is the day that railways repair their track. There have been many occasions when I have waited patiently at my chosen spot for the appearance of a train, only to see a maintenance truck trundling along the line, which meant services have been stopped. Invariably this happened on a Monday, so that is now the day designated for driving long distances and not long waits.

Not wishing to sound like an ageing hippy but there have been good trips and bad trips. The latter are usually caused by being overambitious, a lack of preparation, inclement weather or pure misfortune, and all four combined when I decided to take a trip to New England. My recent trips had been fitted into visits to family

Amtrack GE P32AC-DM arrives at Uttica station with a passenger service from New York.

in Ontario and feeling that I had exhausted Michigan, Wisconsin and the neighbouring states, I looked eastwards to New York, Pennsylvania, Vermont and Maine. It was September, so what better than New England in the fall?

There being no motorways to speak of until Ottawa, it took a day of driving to reach New York State with no railways to see along the way. Another day on the road and I reached my first destination, Woodstock! The site of the 1969 music festival has been designated a National Monument and houses a museum dedicated to the three days of music and peace. I was only forty-nine years too late but 'Man, it was cool!'

From there to Scranton, Pennsylvania, for Steamtown, a large collection of steam locomotives overseen by America's national

Left: The magnificent interior of Uttica station which was going to be demolished by Amtrak until it was rescued by the City for use as offices.

Opposite: Amtrak Siemens ACS-64 crosses the girder bridges over the Connecticut River as it slows to enter Old Saybrook station.

parks, before heading east into New England for the Washington Cog Railway and some lineside activity, but I found very little. Five days of touring the six states yielded a few Amtrak trains, a commuter train and one pickup freight. The weather was for the most part dull, grey and wet. The Washington Cog Railway was shrouded in a heavy mist and pouring rain, fall colours were subdued, mountains hidden by clouds; it was a complete washout, but there's another tick on the bucket list.

As darkness begins to fall, Lackawanna 664 (EMD F3) returns to Steamtown in Scranton from Carbondale with a wine excursion train.

Montana

Fred and I visited Montana during our second trip to the USA. We had been in Sundance, South Dakota, the town that imprisoned Harry Longabaugh for horse stealing and whose name he adopted as an outlaw, watching an American football game between two teams of schoolboys. We were informed by the visiting side supporters that this was a grudge match, a local derby, even though they had travelled 400 miles to get here. We left before the finish for we had several hundred miles to travel ourselves.

Our objective was Yellowstone Park but before that we were going to the site of the Battle of the Little Big Horn where General Custer and 275 cavalrymen lost their lives to the Lakota Sioux and other native tribes led by Crazy Horse. It was the strangest national park I have visited for there was so little to see but so much for the imagination. At the entrance we were given an illustrated brochure and a route to drive which guided us through the stages of the battle. The leaflet brought the conflict to life, as did the markers along the route indicating where a body had fallen, white for the cavalry, red for the Sioux – far more of the former incidentally. The climax came at the 'Last Stand Hill' where the few survivors of the battle met their fate, a cluster of white markers and one with black writing indicating that this was the spot where Custer had fallen. Standing on the top of the hill and gazing at the deserted rolling plains it was so difficult to imagine the violent scenes that had taken place there 150 years before.

There wasn't much railway photography done on this trip but looking at the map I could see that it would be worth visiting Northern Montana and the Marias Pass, and a few years later, I made the first of my two visits in heavy spring snow. Despite the weather I managed to photograph a good selection of trains and vowed to return when the sun was out. The second time was very promising, catching a freight at the top of the pass, followed very quickly by Amtrak's Empire Builder heading for Chicago. Unfortunately, shortly after I had taken a photograph, the train slowed to a stop and didn't move for several hours. Eventually a relief BNSF locomotive appeared from the east and hauled the train away. I photographed it and then headed to Canada, reasoning that everything else on the line had stopped for the rescue. I never returned.

With a raw wind and driving snow it seemed better to remain in the car. BNSF 7321 (GE ES44DC) arrives at a crossing point on Marias Pass with a grain train behind waiting for clearance.

As a snowstorm obscures Glacier National Park BNSF 5167 (GE C44-9W) leads three locomotives with an eastbound grain train.

Goat Lick trestle bridge in the snow with what might well be BNSF 7321 at point with a grain train.

With Glacier National Park obscured by falling snow, a grain train works hard up the grade with BNSF 5180 (GE C44-9W) at the head.

On a perfect day for photography BNSF 5450 (GE C44-9W) and its grain train is reflected in a pool at the summit of Marias Pass.

Pictured against the Glacier National Park and the most photographed barn in the USA, BNSF 5021 (GE C44-9W) comes to the aid of the stranded Empire Builder.

Utah

Of all the thirty-five states that I have driven through, Utah must be my favourite. From the lushness of Zion National Park to the eastern desert, from the weather-beaten rock formations of Arches National Park to the otherworldly pink and white hoodoos of Bryce Canyon, the landscape is astonishing, far removed from anything found in the United Kingdom. There is also plenty of rail traffic to photograph in these amazing settings, courtesy of Union Pacific. The UP line enters the state from Grand Junction, Colorado, via a canyon inaccessible to the ordinary tourist like me, travelling through the desert to Green River where it follows Highway 6 to Provo and Salt Lake City. From there two lines head west; one crosses the Salt Lake on a man-made causeway, again inaccessible due to the rattlesnakes which occupy the western photographic vantage point, the other route runs across salt flats until the Nevada desert is reached at West Wendover.

Two unidentified Union Pacific locomotives cross the desert heading for Green River with the ubiquitous coal train.

Taken from an Interstate rest area on I70, UP 6069 (GE AC44CWCTE) is in charge of a mixed freight heading for Colorado from Green River.

Mesas are a feature of the terrain around Green River and they dominate the skyline as UP 8365 (EMD SD70Ace) heads westwards with another coal train.

UP 5253 (GE AC45CCTE) approaches Green River from the east with a mixed freight bound for Colorado.

UP 8365 once more. Having negotiated Green River, it is heading for Soldier Summit and Salt Lake City.

Above: UP 5253 drifts around the bend into the town of Helper, so named as it once housed locomotives used to push trains over Soldier Summit.

Opposite: UP 5253 emerges from the tunnels at Fork Creek waterfalls. These two pictures illustrate very well my method for finding trains. Find one, follow it.

Above: UP 2592 (GE ET44AC) is at the rear of a train which has taken the branch line towards the mining district of Eccles Canyon.

Opposite: Taken from Kyune Pass Road, UP 5930 (GE AC44CWCTE) catches the late evening sun as it takes its auto train towards Helper.

Above: I discovered this pair with UP 1633 (EMD SD40N) at the front, parked outside a power station to the south of the Great Salt Lake.

Opposite: Having surmounted Soldier Summit, UP 7897 (GE AC45CCTE) begins the long descent to Green River with a coal train.

Above and opposite: West Wendover is an entertainment town, full of hotels and casinos, found parked on the border of Utah and Nevada which is also the dividing line between salt flats and the Nevada desert. This photograph and the one on the following page illustrate an afternoon in the desert. Neither show the lightning bolt that crashed to the earth about a quarter a mile away making the air sizzle and my hair stand on end.

Wyoming

After a day chasing trains at the northern end of Highway 6 in Utah I drove into Wyoming and spent the night in a small town called Evanston which had a building I wanted to visit before I headed for Cheyenne. I found it on the outskirts of the town, amongst mainly deserted rail tracks, the best-preserved Union Pacific roundhouse in the USA, which had been donated to the town council when it was closed by the railroad in 1971.

I wandered inside the half that had already been restored as a convention centre. Although it still retained many of the elements of a roundhouse, I wasn't certain that shiny wooden floors were typical. As I walked around the building, I was approached by a member of staff who asked me, 'Well, how do you like it?' 'It isn't really what I expected,' I replied. 'I thought it would be more railway related, have some old engines or box cars inside.' He laughed, 'It's the council's idea, it is being turned into an asset for the community. There are plans for the remaining half to become a restaurant and a brewery. Ah, here's the boss, she'll tell you more.' A middle-aged blonde lady approached and said 'Hi. Welcome, where are you from?' 'England,' I replied. 'How long are you staying?' she asked. 'I'm here in the States for a fortnight,' I told her. A puzzled look crossed her face, 'What's a fortnight?' The guy I had met first intervened. 'It's an English term. ma'am, means two weeks.' She looked at me, 'Gee, I love your accent,' she said. 'Funny you should say that,' I replied, and went on to recount the story of the two young women in Clinton. When I reached the punch line, she looked at me and said, 'I quite agree.' I hope this doesn't become an audio book!

I drove along Interstate 80 through heavy rain showers and thunderstorms, the scenery changing little until I got near Laramie when the High Plains scrubby look gave way to farmland and rolling hills. The most famous being Sherman Hill between Cheyenne and Laramie. Its steep grade necessitated the building of the Big Boy locomotives to enable freight to be moved more economically before the advent of diesel power. The weather remained very unsettled, as the following pictures will testify.

Opposite: With an unidentified UP locomotive at the rear, a train crosses the salt flats east of West Wendover.

There also appears to be a crock of gold at my hotel as UP 8592 (EMD SD70Ace) pulls out of Cheyenne yard with a westbound auto train.

The view from the Super 8 motel car park. Two unidentified BNSF locomotives are at the rear of a coal train heading for the BNSF yard in Cheyenne.

A stack train catches the evening sun as it runs under the girder bridge carrying BNSF lines with UP 7938 (GE AC4400CW-CTE) in lead position in Cheyenne, Wyoming.

On a back road between Laramie and Cheyenne, unidentified Union Pacific locomotives work hard against the grade with a heavy oil train.

The Laramie Mountains are covered in snow as UP 6866 (GE AC4400CW) approaches the summit of Sherman Hill with a mixed train heading for Cheyenne.

A very heavy storm is over Laramie, though it never reached Tye Siding, where UP 7677 (GE ES44AC) is at the rear of a train going to get very wet, very soon.

The storm is building over Laramie as UP 8310 (EMD SD70Ace), heading for Cheyenne, meets a westbound auto train at Tye Siding, Wyoming.

It is not only along Route 66 that abandoned relics can be seen. UP6004 (GE AC44CWCTE) rolls past a distressed gas station as it heads for Nebraska.

FAILURE (PART II): THE ROAD TO FARGO

If the first example of a failure was due to poor planning, inclement weather and being overambitious, the second was simply bad luck. The first time I went to North Bay, Ontario, I planned a trip into the northern states of the USA. I drove into Michigan from Ontario, on to Wisconsin, across the state to Duluth in Minnesota and finish in North Dakota before returning the same way. The route I chose followed railway tracks for much of the way and Google Earth indicated promising locations for photographs.

The first leg of the trip was from North Bay to the American border at Sault Ste. Marie and roughly followed the route of the Huron Central Railway, but I was unaware then that there was only one train a day each way, both at a time when I wouldn't see them. Undaunted, I drove through Michigan to Green Bay, Wisconsin, where I took in the National Railway Museum before heading across country to Duluth. Railway action was non-existent, so I took a detour to Hibbing, the boyhood home of Bob Dylan. I easily found the house in which he grew up as it was on Bob Dylan Boulevard, though something tells me that this name came later. I took Highway 2 out of Duluth towards Grand Rapids, Michigan, where I saw my first train even though the line had been running alongside the road for miles. This situation continued into North Dakota; nothing at Grand Forks nor at Fargo, so I retraced my steps. I caught a coal train north of Fargo in 70 mph winds. The dust and debris being blown about made driving difficult, but the photograph taken is one of my all-time favourites.

The return journey was the same. Two days of driving to get back to Duluth and one train seen which proved difficult to photograph as it was sitting by a lake, hidden by weeds pretending to be the Ugly Duckling. I took a different route from Duluth; there were no trains, but it was a quicker way back into Michigan and the border. Crossing into Canada I gave my passport to the lady in Border Control, 'Where are you going to go in Canada, sir?' she asked. 'I'm going to North Bay,' I replied. 'What the hell are you going there for?' was her response. My thought was 'what the hell have I been doing?'

Opposite: At Grand Rapids, Minnesota, BNSF 1663 (EMD SD40-2), along with a sister engine, is crossing the Prairie River with a pickup freight.

1689
BNSF
1663
BNSF

5716
5716

Colorado

I am not a fan of large cities. I have been to Denver, Colorado, five times and never been Downtown, but I have been to Coors Field three times to watch the Colorado Rockies play baseball. Fred and I went on our first trip and saw them defeat the St Louis Cardinals in a high-scoring game. We became fans and were thrilled when, later that season, they reached the finals of the World Series only to lose heavily to the Boston Red Sox. Two years on and we were at the ground once more – another victory, this time against the Cincinnati Reds which was marred slightly when a pizza fell from the sky onto Fred's head!

It is at this juncture that I must point out that the Rockies are not a very good side, never having troubled the World Series again, but Fred and I kept the faith. A few years later I was again in the Denver area and decided to go to the game against the San Francisco Giants. I drove to the ground to purchase a ticket and found two ticket office windows open. A guy was buying tickets at one window, so I went to the neighbouring one to buy a ticket. 'Where do you want to sit?' enquired the lady behind the till, showing me a seat map. 'Well, I always sit in that block, so I'll take one there,' I replied. 'That will be 42 dollars.' 'No concessions?' I asked. 'Sure, that will be 21 dollars. Say aren't you from England?' 'I certainly am,' I replied, 'in fact I think you should give me the ticket for free as I have never seen the Rockies lose.' At this point the guy next to me burst into laughter and came across to chat. He was a 'scalper' or a ticket tout and was buying tickets for more important games to sell on. I told him that I had been the season the Rockies had made the World Series. 'If that happens again', he said, 'I'll fly you over as a good luck charm. Say why don't you join me and my wife for a meal in the restaurant tonight? She would love to meet you.' 'You go,' intervened the lady selling tickets, 'It's great up there, good food and a fantastic view of the game.' I declined but said I would join him around the seventh innings, which I did. Sitting down at his table he introduced me to his wife. 'Honey, this is Dave, the guy from England I was telling you about.' I was expecting 'Gee, Dave, I love your accent' but instead she said, 'Hi Dave, pleased to meet you. Do you know the Queen?'

My favourite area in Colorado is Interstate 70 where it dives into Glenwood Canyon. Nearly 20 miles of dual carriageway sharing a narrow gorge with the Colorado River and Union Pacific rails, it is breathtaking. At some points the road going west is above that going east. So restricted is the space that it makes it difficult to photograph trains, but I have found a few vantage points over the years, one of which features in this section. The remaining pictures are taken along the Union Pacific lines that run through the state from Denver to the west.

Opposite: Coal dust is flying from the wagons, joining with the dirt and debris brought by high winds racing across the flat lands of North Dakota. BNSF 5716 (GE AC44CW) heads north at a place Google Earth tells me is Cummings.

Above: Amtrak 822 (GE P40DC), in fortieth anniversary paint scheme, leads the southbound California Zephyr alongside the Colorado River close to Glenwood Springs.

Opposite: Eastbound California Zephyr has left Glenwood Springs and is running along the Colorado River with Amtrak 8 (AMTK 123(P42DC).

Above: UP 7206 (GE AC44CW) with a coal train in the Colorado River Valley at Gypsum.

Opposite: Amtrak 69 AMTK 123(P42DC)) with the eastbound Zephyr in the wonderful Glenwood Canyon just north of Glenwood Springs.

Having left Glenwood Canyon, UP 2648 (GE ES44AC) follows the Colorado River at Dotsero on its eastward journey to Denver.

A meet-up of two coal trains at Tolland. UP 7107 (GE AC44CW) has recently exited from the Moffat tunnel and is heading for Denver, whilst waiting for clearance to head west is UP 5623 (GE AC44CWCTE).

UP 6790 (GE AC44CW) crosses South Boulder Creek at the rear of a coal train heading for the Moffat tunnel.

Wisconsin

A state bounded by water with Lake Michigan to the east and the Mississippi River as the western border. There is plenty of train action on both stretches of waterway: Canadian National are in control of traffic in the east running through to Milwaukee and Chicago, whilst BNSF run trains along the banks of the Mississippi in the west.

First port of call on any of my trips is Green Bay, home to the National Railway Museum which has amongst its collection a Gresley A4, 60008, and advertised to the locals as 'the Eisenhower Train'! Also worth a visit is the magnificent Lambeau Field, home of the Green Bay Packers NFL team. An added bonus is that accommodation, in my experience, is very reasonable compared with some areas of the States. One motel owner explained that he was able to offer a cheap rate most of the year because when the Packers played at home his rates were astronomical, going even higher if the team made the Post-season Playoffs.

The 'Gee, I love your accent' happened here once as I made the mistake of speaking in a large gas station on the outskirts of Oshkosh. The six women on the tills all stopped what they were doing and came over to chat, much to the annoyance of some very burly truckers waiting to get served. Fortunately, my age prevented either side taking things any further.

CN 3030 (GE C40-9W) heads south over the bridge at Oshkosh.

Above: Dodging the shadows heading south, an unidentified BNSF locomotive heads past La Crosse County Park with a coal train.

Opposite: There are many such causeways built along the side of the Mississippi River in Wisconsin. BNSF 6996 (GE ES44C4) is reflected in the still waters of the man-made pond, south of the town of La Crosse.

NS 9450 (GE C40-9W) and helper are reflected in the calm of a backwater of the Mississippi River as they haul an oil train northward.

CN 2883 (GE ES44AC) heads north over the magnificent lifting bridge at Oshkosh with an auto train.

CN 2699 (GE C44-9W) at the head of an oil train crosses the Waupaca River at Decker Memorial County Park. Did I mention that chasing trains is like fishing?